ELIZABETH EVEN, RN

Shift Your Mindset, Your Job, Your Life!

First published by Platypus Publishing 2023

Copyright © 2023 by Elizabeth Even, RN

All rights reserved. No part of this publication may be reproduced, stored or transmitted in any form or by any means, electronic, mechanical, photocopying, recording, scanning, or otherwise without written permission from the publisher. It is illegal to copy this book, post it to a website, or distribute it by any other means without permission.

Elizabeth Even, RN has no responsibility for the persistence or accuracy of URLs for external or third-party Internet Websites referred to in this publication and does not guarantee that any content on such Websites is, or will remain, accurate or appropriate.

Designations used by companies to distinguish their products are often claimed as trademarks. All brand names and product names used in this book and on its cover are trade names, service marks, trademarks and registered trademarks of their respective owners. The publishers and the book are not associated with any product or vendor mentioned in this book. None of the companies referenced within the book have endorsed the book.

First edition

ISBN: 978-1-962133-04-3

Cover art by Mary Ann Smith
Editing by Beck Kettenhofen
Proofreading by Kristin Buishas

This book was professionally typeset on Reedsy.
Find out more at reedsy.com

To John Michael.
Each day we are given is a gift.
This big, crazy family we were lucky enough
to be born into will be with you every step of the way.

Find your why and you will find your way.

                                        John C. Maxwell

Contents

Preface ... ii
Acknowledgement ... vi
Chapter 1 ... 1
Chapter 2 ... 4
Chapter 3 ... 9
Chapter 4 ... 24
Chapter 5 ... 38
Chapter 6 ... 49
Chapter 7 ... 64
Chapter 8 ... 87
About the Author ... 89

Preface

Introduction...

Yo, bedside nurses. Join this committee, get certified, and go back to school...

Sound familiar? Do you want to get paid more for doing this? Pfft. But if you play your cards right, you might get 'exceeds' on your evaluation which would bump your annual merit increase by at least eighty-two cents. Cool? Oh, and your PTO for the summer was denied because we have three people out on maternity leave. What about February?

What is a nurse to do? Well, it's time to flip the script and think outside the box. You are holding a degree in what may be the most versatile profession on planet Earth. There's a smorgasbord out there and who said you can only choose one thing? I have been a nurse for close to twenty years and although I have primarily been in the ER, my roles there have changed several times throughout the years. For four years I had four different jobs and it was the perfect solution for me at the time. I wasn't working any more hours than I had been previously, but I was making more money, was less burnt out, and was in complete control of my schedule which was the priority for me at the time because of my young family. I felt like I had cracked the code in many ways and have never looked back.

I absolutely love taking care of patients, but now I do so much more on my own terms. I feel this is why I have been able to stay at the bedside for as long as I have while continuing to challenge myself outside of the hospital.

It's time to ask yourself what you actually want to be doing and why.

Here I have laid out an incredibly simple framework for you with examples and exercises to ignite ideas for where you want to go next as well as exactly how you are going to get there. After reading this book, you will have lots of ideas along with a plan of action.

Also, congratulations! Most people have not even moved beyond the daily complaining stage to even take the first step. Just by picking up this book you are ahead of most other people. Be proud of yourself. Getting started is the hardest part and you can check that right off your list.

Before I end this section, I wanted to sincerely **THANK YOU** for being here and reading. I cannot say that enough. As a first-time author, it means the world to me – it truly does.

May this book be the spark you need to get out there and crush all kinds of goals – and when you do, I want to hear all about it. Drop me a line at hello@straighttalkrn.com. It will be my favorite email of that day – that is a guarantee.

You've got this!

How to get the most from this book...

This book is intended to be a quick read that is both thought-provoking and actionable. It is written in a way that lets you start with any section that speaks to you. Perhaps you are interested in first reading about goals and action. Please, start there! Perhaps you have goals and have taken some action but have not yet achieved what you set out to do, and maybe you've been down that road more than once already. The accountability and self-reflection sections are great places to start.

For all of my grumpy folks who feel like they are forever stuck in their situation, starting from the beginning 'Mindset' chapter is a must. No matter where you start, my advice would be to read the whole book (come on, you can do it in one afternoon) and then focus on one thing to implement in your life. Yes, you read that correctly – one. Give it time. When that one thing becomes a true habit and second nature to you, or you have crossed that goal off of your list, you can add another action into the mix.

After all, we all know what happens when you try to change everything at once. This is it! You say you are going to change your life! You are going to get up early every day and go for a run, and then you are going to come home and whip up a smoothie you read all about on Instagram. Then there's this meal service you just know will be the answer to eating healthy, and what about that new skincare line that you have a promo code for...

Well, we know what is likely to happen. After a few weeks of enthusiasm, it becomes more difficult, or even impossible, to stick with all of these changes. You never have all the ingredients you need for the smoothie. The meal service requires so much prep work. It only takes a few derailments or days where things don't work out for one of these new habits to fall by the wayside, soon followed by another and likely another.

We as human beings cannot handle changing multiple things at once, not well anyway. For more on this, there is a book I highly recommend – *Organize Tomorrow Today* by Dr. Jason Selk. It's a fantastic book about action – I walked away with several new habits (although I truly started with just one) that I have found incredibly helpful in my own life, not to mention he is a force of nature. I reached out to him before I started to write this to ask if I could include some of his concepts in my book and not only did he reply within a few hours, but his reply could not have been more supportive. I've included it in the accountability section. If you walk away from reading this with one new mindset change or a new habit that you have incorporated into your life, I consider that a true success.

Remember – you didn't get here overnight, and your entire life will not change overnight, either. It is a process that takes time, consistency, and repeated action. Let's get started, shall we?

Acknowledgement

Special Thanks

The encouragement and support that I have received while on this journey has been so incredible and humbling. From the very early planning stages all the way through publishing I cannot thank my friends and family enough. My husband, Charles, for his support every step of the way and for feigning interest even when everything I wanted to tell him was at the exact moment he was trying to go to bed. To my mom, Mary, for *almost* picking the winning title, my dad, John and brother, James for their text support, and my twin sister, Kristin, English teacher extraordinaire for getting through my rough draft while asking me over and over what my problem with spacing and commas was.

To my partner in crime, my sounding board, and the best motivator and neighbor on the planet. Kristen, this whole thing would not be off the ground without your encouragement and support, and you know it. Thanks for listening to me FOR YEARS about this. The Universe did me a solid when it brought you next door. To many more years of WB magic.

To my cousin John Michael. Life is about making that lemonade. Your journey has inspired me to not waste a moment as none of them are promised. I cannot wait to toast to your health and strength someday soon. Annmarie- our family is in awe of you and cannot thank you enough for taking care of John during this time and always. We love you!

To my beta readers! Paul, Steph, Susie, Alexis, Jenny, K-boogie. You had to get through this without any of the commas that Paul and Kristin added. I know it wasn't easy, but you were very kind about it and offered some fantastic suggestions as well as some much-needed encouragement. From the very bottom of my heart- thank you all.

To Dr. Jason Selk- for being so generous with your information and for the words of encouragement that served as a motivation to make it to the finish line with my first book. I cannot tell you how many times I have reminded myself to own my day instead of letting it own me through the principles of Organize Tomorrow Today. That book was life-changing and one I will refer to often.

Beck! My editor and word wizard! I cannot thank you enough for cutting out chunks that had no business in being there, not quitting immediately when I told you that I accidentally sent you my very FIRST version which you painstakingly worked on for DAYS, and for generally making this book better for everyone that picks it up. I cannot thank you enough.

To Mary Ann Smith, my cover designer. You took all of my ideas and made them into something so much better than I could have ever imagined. You were so wonderful and flexible and responsive and supportive. Seeing the cover for the first time was the moment I felt like "This is really happening- this is a real book!" Thank you.

To Matt Rudnitsky for his 'Punchy Books Accelerator' class, which taught me everything I needed to know to be a first-time author (which was everything). Your videos and style were exactly what I needed- thank you!

And finally....**to all my nurses.** The love that I have for all of you is simply unmatched. The work that we do is so incredibly important and often completely taken for granted. We touch the lives of strangers in a way that only those in the field would understand. For those of you that I know personally, you know that I am your number one supporter and always in your corner. For those of you whom I do not- thank you for all you do for your patients and the profession. We are all better and stronger when we *take care of and support* one another. It's tough out there, but we are tougher. I love hearing all of the stories about nurses out there straight-up making moves, making it happen and making a difference! May you never lose that fire and passion and may you never settle!

xoxoxo,

Liz

Chapter 1

My story. The early days.

Before my last semester of nursing school, we were asked to rank our top hospitals and nursing units where we would like to spend our last semester and complete our end-of-the-program project. Decisions would be made by way of a lottery. Seemingly unlucky, I "won" my last choice for both the hospital (the one that was the farthest away) as well as the nursing unit. I hated cardiac in school but I was assigned to a cardiovascular-thoracic step-down unit at a hospital in the city. Fast forward to many years since and this truly ended up being the best thing that could have happened to me. I ended up at a large, academic medical center with fantastic nurses who were actually nice to me as a student. (To all of my nurses on the old 16 West – thank you all so much, you were truly fantastic!) I didn't realize it until many years later, but the universe was looking out for me with those lottery results. After the semester ended, I ended up staying there as a new grad and have been working at that hospital ever since.

Looking back, there were so many opportunities there that simply would not have been available at a local community hospital. I signed up for a Master's Degree in Nursing Administration about a year later, knowing that the longer I waited, the less likely it would be I actually did it. Six months later, I applied for a formal charge role, but was told that I wasn't quite ready yet. Discouraged and a little restless, I took a chance and followed Lauren, my work bestie into a place I had no intention of ever working – the emergency department (cue dreadful music).

It was so hard for me to leave my first nursing unit because I *loved* my co-workers, but it was very specific and it was the same stuff over and over again and I didn't want to pigeonhole myself so early in my career. Of course, once I joined Lauren in the ER, she left me a hot second later to be a travel nurse in California and I *knew* she was never coming back. I had them write "You are ruining my life" on her farewell cake and I was right. Fifteen years later, she is still in San Diego, but at least I now have a reason to visit there as often as I can.

The ER is a tough place full of long-time nurses and big personalities. When I arrived, I was 24 years old and a little sassy. (Apologies and thanks to all of my co-workers for putting up with me back then). After some typical new kid growing pains, I eventually fell in love with the department and felt like I was truly home.

There are *so many* skills that you have to use in the ER. With a wide knowledge base, loads of technical skills, crucial conversations, and *a lot* of PR – the ER really had it all. I was challenged daily and I loved that. I finally got that leadership role I had been aiming for, only to have it taken away about eighteen months later when the hospital restructured the entire position.

Again, I found myself at a crossroads. What next? On one hand, I didn't want to take a step back into regular staffing as I had finally taken that step forward. On the other hand, I didn't want to leave the ER I now loved and all of its craziness.

CHAPTER 1

What follows in these chapters are the steps that I took to find my next challenge. I have now used these steps on multiple levels and multiple times over the years. If variety is the spice of life, nursing is the entire spice rack!

I hope that these simple steps help you as they have helped me and many colleagues that I have talked to over the past twenty years. I urge you to stick with it, not give up, and to **do the work** it takes to get you wherever you need to go.

If nursing teaches us anything, it is that we only get one crack at this thing called life. I want to squeeze all I can out of mine and my hope for you is that you do the same.

Chapter 2

How did we get here?

When I first got my nursing degree in 2004, there was a huge push for nurses to go back to school and get their advanced degrees. Perhaps this started long before that, but I remember that it was all we heard about from managers, from advertisements, you name it. It was always something like: "When you are going to '*advance your degree?*'"

And it worked! It seemed that more nurses were going back to school than ever before. Nowadays, it's hard to find a nurse with more than three years of experience who is not in school for some sort of advanced degree. And what did all these nurses go back for? For the ones who had a plan and knew what they wanted, they may be doing something that they find challenging, that they enjoy, and are making a decent living doing so. Others that I have talked to are graduating soon or have just finished but are less happy about the pay and the schedules they are hearing about in job interviews. But what about those who are not sure if they want to go back to school? Not sure what they want to do next? Time and time again, I see nurses go back to school feeling like they need to do *something* and graduate in the same boat but with more debt, more responsibility, and a few more initials after their name. The key is to try to ask yourself if your destination aligns with your **'why'** before starting.

CHAPTER 2

What can you do if you are not sure? First, we need to figure out where this feeling that you need to be doing something different is even coming from. Those feelings of unrest should be listened to. That uneasiness is the universe trying to help you out. These are signs that it is time for a true change, and it is up to you to not only recognize them but act upon them. I truly believe that one of the reasons I am in such a happy and balanced place today is because I listened to the universe and have not been afraid to explore possible next steps, take a few leaps of faith and say "Hey, why not?!" Although it can be scary, it can also be very liberating because you have control over the decisions that you make. Not sure? Take a small step. Feeling adventurous? Take a leap. Spoiler alert! You will not always choose right. Even when you do, life is not like the movies where you are guaranteed a "happily ever after." But real life, with all of its struggles and opportunities, in the end is so much better than the movies, especially when you are looking in your rearview at how far you have come, and all of the struggles and challenges you have conquered. What a sense of accomplishment!

Overall, a big part of all of this is your mindset and the lens through which you view each and every day. We will talk about that in the next chapter.

When you listen to your gut and take action, you are training your mind and yourself to break free from old ways of complacent thinking and decision-making. This is our one and only life and you are a *nurse!*
Do you realize what that means?! That degree with your name on it is like your own personal golden ticket.

First and foremost, you are *essential*. Do not ever forget that or let anyone make you feel less than that. During the Covid pandemic, when everyone was staying home and thousands of people lost their jobs, you know who the world turned to? Us. The longer I have been a nurse the more I appreciate the universal and profound profession of nursing. The variety and job security that come with a nursing degree is unparalleled to any other job on the planet in my experience.

There are *thousands* of possibilities out there, meaning there is absolutely *no* reason to stay in a job you hate for twenty or more years just to inch toward retirement and *then* really start your life.

Do me a favor. Look up any nurse leader – one you have seen at a conference, perhaps. I bet they all have one thing in common. They have all held a myriad of different roles during their careers at different hospitals or companies. Variety is an excellent teacher, and every job and new place shows you something new. Some will be a great fit, and others may be a giant disaster, but from every one of them, you will walk away with some new tools in your toolbox, a little more experience, and a better idea of what feeds your soul and what you can *definitely* do without.

So, let's get down to business. We have talked about it, but what is *it*? It's not rocket science or magic. It's not a quick fix or a miracle. It's a tool similar to a shovel. Without picking it up and using it, it is worthless.

So how do you use it? Well, that is the great part – it is crazy simple and gets easier with practice. Eventually, you may not even realize you are doing it! I call her, The Enlightened Action Pyramid© (EAP).

CHAPTER 2

Straight Talk, RN LLC - ©2022

As you can see, the reflection step is the star of the show. I feel this step is crucial to the entire process as well as the **most** overlooked. Some people naturally tend towards self-reflection, while others can't seem to do this to save their lives. Getting in touch with yourself – checking in with yourself – to see how things are going, in my opinion, is crucial and should be a regular part of your mental wellness plan whether you love your job or not.

We will talk much more about this in the coming sections, but the EAP is not a step-by-step ladder, but rather a framework that you may use to build good mental habits for long-term decision-making and career planning.

I decided on a pyramid because without accountability, progress falls apart, and without self-reflection, we are moving forward without a map.

Although we are using this tool for careers, it can be used by nurses and non-nurses alike for any big life-changing decision.

Before we jump into the pyramid, though, we need to set the stage for success and talk about our mindset as this influences absolutely everything we do each and every day.

Chapter 3

MINDSET – You control your mental narrative.

"Being challenged in life is inevitable, being defeated is optional."
— Roger Crawford

Key Points & Takeaways:

- How you choose to look at something is eighty percent of the battle.
- Do you tend to rock out sunglasses or rose-colored ones?
- The sooner you realize that you control the narrative in your brain, the better off you will be.
- Mindset and gratitude are incredibly intertwined. Be equally attentive to both.

There is an old adage about two shoe salesmen who were sent to Africa to assess the shoe market. When they arrived, they were shocked to see that not one person was wearing shoes. They went to a few other towns and then prepared two very different reports to send back to headquarters. One salesman reported, "This place is a bust. There's no potential because nobody wears shoes." The other salesman said just the opposite. He exclaimed, "This is a goldmine! We are the first! No competition. Send inventory."

This story is a great example to highlight how mindset can shape our actions. These two salesmen were looking at the exact same thing but saw it in two very different ways. This highlights a choice all of us have every day in every situation, and that choice is our mindset.

In order for us to get the most out of the enlightened action pyramid, we must be aware of our mindset. Mindset is eighty percent of the battle and nobody likes wasting time. We need to get our minds in the right place to move forward and that is true of every moment of every day. Therefore, perspective is where we will always begin.

Let's do a quick self-assessment. On a daily basis, do you tend to view your day through rose-colored glasses, or are you more of a sunglasses type of person? More often than not, is your cup half full or half empty? Do you tend to complain about little things, or brush off those small annoyances and instead focus on the big picture?

If you are in the rose-colored camp as your default setting, great – that will help you a lot in this life because no matter what your mindset is, you *are* going to work that Saturday morning, even though it is a dark, cold and angry winter day in Chicago and all you want to do is stay in your warm bed.

Now, I'm not saying you have to wake up and have your own Disney-esque scene with song and dance as you get into the shower with birds chirping to the music in the background, but you *own* your mindset. If you feel like you don't, you have some work to do. You are in the right place- keep reading.

CHAPTER 3

I speak from experience on this one: in my teens and twenties, nothing was *ever* my fault. I used to say, "I can't help how I feel" as a cop-out. I look back at those years and just want to shake my younger self and tell her how silly (and frankly, annoying) she sounds. You can't control what is in your own mind?! Of course, you can. It may just take a conscious effort in the beginning and a lot of consistency to do so, but you absolutely can. While in some ways it may be comforting to feel like you are not in control and therefore not responsible, on the flip side, this mindset can also leave you feeling powerless and lost. That is *not* where we want to be.

So, let's get to work figuring out our life plan! Yeah, okay, cool, let's do that. Long pause. Longer pause...

Okay, so how do we start? Yep. I know. This feeling of where to start is very familiar. You hear the universe in your gut but now you need to figure out the message. It's a feeling, a thought, something that happens to you. It's what they mean when they say "open your eyes" to the possibilities. The fact that you have recognized there is something in your gut is step one. This in itself is not always easy when we are busy and distracted and tend to put ourselves after our children/families, our jobs, and even our pets or gardens. We will talk more about routinely checking in with ourselves in the self-reflection chapter, but for now, let's say we have recognized the signal that it may be time for a change. You now have a choice to either listen to that or ignore it with the chance you may slowly get crabby and stuck. That last option sounds like a real hoot. This initial recognition is one of the earliest times that mindset comes into play.

There is a reason that this entire chapter on mindset precedes the discussion about The Enlightened Action Pyramid ©. If mindset were in the pyramid picture, it would be a giant bubble around the whole thing because it surrounds every facet of the process. Yes, it's *that* important!

A Mindset Exercise...

I want to share a story from my own life where a simple shift in perspective made a big difference.

Back in the day, we had a nurse who I felt didn't particularly love me. To be honest, I don't think she even really *liked* me all that much! I don't blame her for this – she came from the school of OG ER nurses and I was a twenty-four-year-old sassy newbie. You get the picture.

Fast forward a year or so and she became my manager. Knowing that she would do my reviews and she now had a direct impact on my work life, I asked if we could have a meeting to discuss things. During the meeting, I essentially told her that I got the feeling she didn't like me much and she basically told me that I wasn't wrong and that I was a bit of a hotshot. Welp. At least I knew it wasn't all in my head!

Years later, she and I ended up working in the same circle, but now in new jobs. I was still struggling with how to best interact with her. My mental loop was anything other than positive or useful. I dreaded having to have any interaction with her and tiptoed around trying to avoid her. It was awful.

Then one day, I had an epiphany.

I have loved reading Harvard Business Review articles about leadership, and many of those articles talked about emotional intelligence: ways to grow emotionally as a leader and deal with difficult people and situations.

CHAPTER 3

Eventually, it clicked – that is *exactly* what I had in front of me. I had the ultimate difficult person/situation that I could *learn* from and therefore overcome. I thought to myself, *"Liz, you are not a small personality. There is no doubt that you are going to have to work with people who do not like you or who are challenging in some way many times throughout your career. What you have in front of you is the ultimate real-life practice to figure this out and be successful."*

From that moment on, everything changed. As soon as I made that mental shift, the stuff that used to send me into a destructive mental loop instead challenged me to figure out how to manage through it with the leader's mind I knew I had. I did not confront her on the fact that I felt she wasn't my number one fan. Remember, I had already sat down with her once and knew enough about where we stood. Instead, I kept my cool, put my professional hat on, and went about my job. I stopped avoiding her and met the situation head-on.

The results were nothing short of miraculous for me. My stress and anxiety about seeing her at work were gone. Yes, I still got butterflies when I saw her or had to interact with her, but comments that I had previously felt were passive-aggressive (whether she intended them to be or not) were now viewed as excellent real-life practice opportunities.

The situation with her instead morphed into an exciting professional puzzle to solve and I no longer took things personally. Real or imagined, the fact is, that a simple mindset shift made a world of difference for me. I stopped giving someone else any power over me and felt like I walked away with a very impactful real-life learning situation under my belt.

I have often dug down and thought about how I handled that situation throughout the years and have talked to many colleagues about similar situations. I urge them to shift their own mindsets. Because at the end of the day, there was only one simple change that happened. Neither of us changed jobs – the *only* thing that changed was my mindset.

After that, my actions followed suit and the rest is history.

Mindset Exercise – Working a twelve on a Saturday:

Let's say you have to go to work on a Saturday and you are very resentful about it. I get it. I also hate working on Saturdays and have felt this way many times. Oh, and it is *beautiful* outside. And, of course, you are working twelve hours. Okay, yep, this situation appears to be all negative. But you are going to clock in if you are resentful or not and it would be a much nicer day for you (as well as all your co-workers) if you reset your mindset before the start of your shift.

Despite what we may think sometimes, we control our internal narrative. We have the gift of active thought. You could be having a negative thought and you can actually tell yourself to stop and fill in the blank with what you want to be thinking about instead.

It is *your* mind. Take control of it. There is a subconscious, of course, but similar to the concepts taught in cognitive behavioral therapy taught at Harvard University, [EE2] reframing your negative thoughts with positive ones can actually make you mentally and physically feel better. On the commute to that Saturday shift, you are going to stop the hamster wheel of hating your job and having to work on Saturdays, and fill in the blank with something more productive.

Here are a few examples – pick your favorite.

- I'm thankful for this job and the paycheck that comes with it.
- I have great co-workers and am thankful to have them on weekends to hang out with.
- Even though I'm working on Saturday, I like having a job where I have some weekdays off because it allows me to attend to things for my kids, run errands, and [insert your thing here].

On the flip side, you can also use this Saturday angst to fuel a change if you truly feel like it is time. This could look like any of the following:

- It's time to look for a Monday-Friday job. No more weekends or holidays for me.
- I'm listening to my gut and it is time for a change. I'm going to talk to a few folks to figure out the next steps.
- I'm going to apply for school and when I graduate, I will accept a job where I am not required to work weekends ever again. BOOM!
- I'm going to pursue a side hustle that does not require weekend work and go per diem or part-time at my current job.

Whatever your situation is, take back control of your mental narrative. *Own it. Use it* – to either get in a better head space or as motivation to make a change.

Mindset vs. Channel Capacity…

One important concept we need to discuss when it comes to mindset is channel capacity, which Dr. Jason Selk discusses in detail in his book.

The concept itself is simple. Research has shown us [EE1] over and over again, that we as humans do not multitask very well. Most people completely disagree with this, thinking they do a great job of multitasking every day, but countless studies have proven the contrary. Oh, we *can do* multiple things at once (and we do), but that does not mean that we do them all *well*. One factor that makes an enormous difference is how new and/or complicated the task or situation is. Driving is a great example. You may or may not remember your early days of driving a car, but everything was new, and your brain was actively processing everything from ensuring your seatbelt was put on correctly, to checking your mirrors, figuring out where the turn signal was, and so on. Your brain was entirely focused on this new experience and could not actively process anything else at the same time, therefore you had met channel capacity and your brain was capped. Fast forward a few years and now you can get in the car and drive somewhere familiar and seriously not use one active brain cell. Your brain is no longer completely engaged in that task; therefore you can likely focus on something else during that time much more effectively.

Think about your first nursing clinical or your first nursing job. Talk about channel capacity! You were likely so focused on the many tasks that you needed to complete each day while simultaneously trying to focus on and retain all the information you were being told from your preceptor and your patients, that you likely felt as though your brain might explode at any moment.

In the early days of my first nursing job, I had about a twenty-minute bus ride back to my apartment and I would straight up fall asleep on the way home. I even missed my stop a time or two! I had never done this before or since. I was *exhausted*.

Fast forward about two years and I was itching for my next move. I felt as though I wasn't being challenged anymore due to how specific my unit was, and the whole process was on an autopilot of sorts. My brain was no longer overwhelmed like in those early days.

In light of all of this information, Dr. Selk strongly urges us to tackle *one* thing at a time which flies in the face of how most humans live their lives. I am guilty of this myself. I frequently remind myself of what my priorities are for the day (cough, cough, get this book written and published) and try to ensure those get done *first*.

There may be a "right time," but likely never a perfect one...

The point of all of this in terms of your career is this: you may have your rose-colored glasses on and a fantastic mindset, but the timing just may not be right due to channel capacity. I spoke to a woman recently who was feeling very lost in her career and knew that she was currently not in the right place. She also mentioned that she and her husband were just beginning to explore IVF (in vitro fertilization) to try to get pregnant. Given the fact that she has a job, is getting paid, and has health insurance, her priority is *not* finding a new job right now. It's on growing her family and navigating everything that comes with that.[1]

There are many examples of when channel capacity is maxed: a new health diagnosis, young children, a recent move, etc. Recognizing when this is the case is important because sometimes it can be a little unclear, or you could more accurately be dealing with a mindset issue instead of a channel capacity issue.

Let me break this down using an example. You have been working on your unit for three years now and you feel like it's time for a change, but you're not sure what you want to do next. You are relied upon heavily by your boss and essentially run the entire clinic. You know that if you left, they would all basically be screwed as nobody knows what you do.

– You may have realized it, but this is not channel capacity.

This would be more of a mindset issue because nothing is holding you back aside from you feeling guilty that you would be leaving your current boss and clinic. Let me tell you something that initially made me sad, but also ended up taking some weight off my mental shoulders at the same time. Many years ago, I dislocated my shoulder while surfing in San Diego. When I got back home about a week later, I showed up for work and they said I couldn't work without a doctor's note saying I was cleared to return. I felt so guilty because of course the department was crazy busy, but Jennifer, the very seasoned charge nurse said, "Listen crazy girl, don't worry about it. This place will always be this place. It will be fine." And you know what? Fifteen years later, she's still right. Still there. Still seeing 100,000 patients a year, even with all the nurses that have come and gone throughout the years.

Although some things have remained constant, healthcare, in general, has changed *so much* over the last fifteen years. It has had to adapt in countless ways. Although I feel there are many aspects of great care that have been all but lost over the years, that ER is still there, doing the best she can. It didn't fall apart without me. It's like traveling the world and finding yourself feeling very small in relation to the planet all of a sudden. It's a powerful juxtaposition of feeling tiny and empowered all at the same time.

Wherever you are working now will, be, fine. That is not to take away the great work that you do there but don't let that root you to the ground, either.

CHAPTER 3

Gratitude and mindset are closely related concepts.

It's safe to say everybody knows what gratitude is, but not everybody knows how they benefit from it. There have been countless studies about the correlation between feeling grateful and improved health such as a UCLA study [EE3] that has shown it can lower your blood pressure, heart rate and breathing to help with overall relaxation. Feeling grateful for what you currently have or the life you currently lead while striving to always challenge and improve yourself is what I feel life is all about! The important thing is to be intentional with it, especially if you are more likely to see the glass as half-empty, you will benefit the most from practicing it often.

You have likely seen ads for apps with names like "Gratitude Garden", or "Three good things" that prompt users to feel grateful by asking them to write down or think about specific things. If you need a boost in this area, find one that resonates with you and incorporate it into your everyday life. You don't need to spend any money, and you do not need to write anything down if you really don't want to, but it helps, especially if you are in a place in life that you are desperate to get out of. You know yourself. Pick something that is a good fit that you can stick with. The sticking with it is the most important part. The plan is that eventually, it becomes a habit, then second nature, and then just a part of who you are and how you think. If gratitude becomes second nature to you, I promise you that life will look so much better through those rose-colored glasses and you will be so happy that you set out on this journey.

When I was younger, my grandma gave me a little notebook and told me to write down anything that made me smile. I was in high school at the time, so of course I smiled and just threw it in my bag to not touch it again for years. One day I decided to give it a try. It was this tiny 3-inch notebook that lived in my bag and went everywhere with me. I started jotting down a few words when I would see something that made me smile or get that warm, happy feeling. For example, I drove by a group of little kids in a park who were playing soccer. One of them had just scored a goal and they screamed "Goooooooooooal!" like a professional announcer. That made me smile. Wrote that down. Once, after a breakup, I was driving down the street when a gust of wind blew a huge swarm of leaves in this awesome pattern that looked like an ocean wave doing ballet. I wrote that down, too. Over time, I started adding more detail so that I could remember each moment perfectly even years later. That was over twenty years ago. To this day, when I look back at those tiny pages, I am taken back to that moment and I smile all over again. Try making a smile book of your own. It costs nothing to start and, in the end meant everything to keep.

A more recent gratitude example from my own life is that I have always hated waking up early. I have had to do so for work most of my life, until recently when I started working primarily from home. Now in the morning, I often take time to sit down on a chair by my window as the sun is coming up, have a few sips of coffee, and simply take a few minutes to feel incredibly grateful that I am not already showered, dressed and out of the house before my kids even open their eyes, as I have been for countless years before. Instead, I get to see them off to school and walk back into a quiet house to log on to my computer to start my workday. Need I say more? Or the fact that I can get outside and go for a quick run on my lunch break because it doesn't matter that my face is the shade of a ripe tomato when I am done...

The moments that make you feel this way are very personal but find whatever they are in your life – and then find more of them! This is my story. These are *my* priorities. I urge you to think about yours.

CHAPTER 3

What is most important to you? What are you grateful for?

Feeling grateful every day even in small ways is one of the best ways to train your brain and therefore your mindset for growth, happiness, and success. Success is the way *you* define it. After all, who cares about any other definition?

If you take away anything from this book, I hope it's this. A small change might just relieve stress and make you happier; it did for me. If you are a glass half empty person, I urge you to make this your priority this year and set out on your gratitude journey with intention. You won't regret it. Find something or someone to hold you accountable. Share your intention with others. Saying it out loud or writing it down will heighten your chances of achieving a goal. Over time, these simple actions become invaluable and powerful fuel for your positive mindset.

Give yourself the credit you deserve...

We are our own worst critics. We have talked a lot about mindset in our lives and situations, but what about our mindset towards ourselves? A few years ago, my company asked me if I would review something that they were going to post about human trafficking. Although I was happy to help, my inner dialogue was, "I don't want to come off as some human-trafficking expert when I'm not." Sure, I worked in ER and we received education and training about this, but I didn't consider myself an *"expert"* in the subject.

I called a physician friend of mine who is often interviewed on the news for various medical topics and he said to me, "Liz, you have just uncovered the secret of academia. There is no 'certificate' for these types of things, no classes. They are going to publish that piece whether you review it or not. Likely, it was written by a non-clinician and you have far more context and experience that makes you an expert compared to your peers at your company."

I reviewed it and was happy to see that he was right. While it was well written, it was obvious that it was not written by a clinician. The team was very thankful for my nurse's eye on the piece, and I was happy to have contributed to what I feel was a very important topic to cover. Everyone wins.

When I thought about writing this book or even starting my company, my self-doubt reared its head. I thought "What if they don't like what you have to say? Who are *you* to write a book?!" After all, it seemed that in every book I picked up, the author had the most impressive resume on the planet.

"Coached thousands of C-Suite employees to greatness!"

"Worked with major league baseball players to get them to the World Series mindset!"

"Was the CNO of this gigantic hospital system and author of five international best-sellers!"

You get the picture.

One of the pieces of advice I have heard Sara Blakely say was to turn something you think is a weakness into a strength.

The writing class for new authors that I signed up for pointed out this

CHAPTER 3

same concept, as did Pat Flynn from Smart Passive Income. [EE4]

They all echoed the same sentiment, in that sometimes, the best person to learn from is the person who is a few steps ahead of you, *not* the expert who has been doing this for forty years and simply cannot remember all the small things anymore.

It's like a twenty-year nurse trying to teach a new graduate nurse. You forget what you didn't know when you were a new grad.

So, here I am. Possibly a few steps ahead of you, showing you what I know to help you over the bridge, and up the rung.

My arm is extended – grab hold.

[1] A shout-out to all those reading this book who are struggling to grow their families. You are not alone. It took me seven pregnancies and lots of stressful years to have my three children and I would not wish that anxiety on anyone. Stay strong and try to take care of yourself through all of this. Having a support network to talk to can help :)❤

[EE1]https://www.npr.org/2008/10/02/95256794/think-youre-multitasking-think-again#:~:text=As%20technology%20allows%20people%20to,do%20lots%20of%20things%20simultaneously.

[EE2]https://sdlab.fas.harvard.edu/cognitive-reappraisal/positive-reframing-and-examining-evidence

[EE3]https://www.uclahealth.org/news/health-benefits-gratitude#:~:text=Taking%20a%20moment%20to%20be,to%20help%20with%20overall%20relaxation.

[EE4]www.spi.com

Chapter 4

Accountability- The Good Time Governor

"The dream is free. The hustle is sold separately."
– Tyrese Gibson

Key Points & Takeaways:

- Nobody is going to do this for you.
- Find your support system – the *right* one for this kind of stuff.
- Are you an internal or external processor?
- None of this is one and done – accountability is for life.
- Give yourself a lot of grace but go easy on the slack.

If mindset was eighty percent, here comes the other twenty percent right here and one of the main reasons why people do not achieve their goals.

I have talked to *so many* great nurses who are amazing but feel stuck and it hurts my soul to watch them waste years without making any sort of change. Their reasons are always the same: "I can't." (Fill in the blank). They have a reason or excuse for every suggestion as to why it will not work. Well then, you know what I say? You are one hundred percent

CHAPTER 4

right. It will *not* work. They have already failed simply because they have already given up before they even started. And why is this?

It might be they are looking at a giant elephant that has been standing there for years and it seems so overwhelming that they believe there is no way they can get past it. I have looked at my own elephant many times. But, as they say, the way to eat an elephant is one bite at a time. Nobody can take that bite for you; you have to pick up the fork yourself.

This book can be your fork. At the end of the day, if you do not pick up the fork, this will be a nine-dollar fork that got you nowhere. That is the thing about any advice. Without action, it is all just words. It's like reading a book about budgeting because you feel like you never have enough money and then not changing a single spending habit after you acquire it. Darn it! More money wasted.

[EE2]

Even though you may not always feel like it or find it fun, you are a grown-up now and have to hold yourself accountable. There are likely no more coaches, teachers, or parents on your back about your day-to-day activities.

For some to change, it seems they have to be so miserable that they've hit rock bottom, but that is such an awful place to be for any length of time. I would like you to realize that these bites of your elephant could be so simple and small that at first, you might not even realize that you are taking them. You are taking bites right now by reading this book. You have already started your journey and are in the small percentage of people who are doing something about feeling unhappy. Keep going.

One of my favorite trainers, Senada Greca, says in one of her workout videos, "Discipline takes over when motivation doesn't show up." This is important, because let's be serious, you are not going to wake up each and every day motivated to kick ass for the rest of your life. This is where having a goal and a plan are crucial. If you know specifically what you need to get done that day to be successful, you are much more likely to succeed. For example, you need to come down and spend 90 minutes editing your book. If you are pushing yourself towards a goal you are passionate about, you can use that passion *and direction* to win more battles with yourself, but here's the thing about consistency. The side-by-side comparison looks like little to no progress, so it is easy to give up. It's like those home-improvement shows - they show up to a house and have it gutted and transformed into this awesome new space – all in the span of thirty minutes!

In reality, this took *months* of super boring and labor-intensive work. Since that's not the most entertaining television, they skip to the good part – the transformation and the big reveal!

Inspiration – Surround yourself with people who are out there doing amazing things...

[EE3]

Find and follow people who inspire you to improve yourself or your situation. By now, you know that I am inspired by Sara Blakely, as I think she is a fantastic role model for women (especially in business). She spent two years single-handedly selling Spanx once she finally got into a few stores – which took years. For *years* she was spending eight or more hours a day in hosiery departments *straight-up* hustling. She was flying to all these stores by herself, sleeping in hotels, talking to the executives, the people that worked there, and every single shopper that came within a few yards of her.

With success and confidence like hers, you might think she never wondered if she was going to make or if all of this effort was worth it, but just like the rest of us, she did. Like the countless videos online of body transformations that chronicle where they started and where they are now. Again, the videos are only about 15 seconds long but think about that true timeline. *Years*. You don't think there were countless days, especially in the beginning where they wanted to skip or just give up altogether? You better believe there were! This is where small goals on the way to larger ones are so important. Without them, losing all motivation and giving up is so much more common. You need to have some small wins that make you feel like you have accomplished something, which then feeds into your motivation and keeps you going forward.

If something is important to you, it is up to you to prioritize it, break it into pieces, and find the time to get it done.

An example of this is when I signed up to run my first marathon. I downloaded a free training guide that laid out what I needed to do to prepare and the question changed from, "Am I going to run today?" to "*When* am I going to run today?"

It *was* happening. I *was* running. This mindset shift was crucial. I had just had my first baby six months prior, and to say I was nowhere near ready would have been incredibly accurate. This is why we break bigger goals into small manageable chunks that are less intimidating and more manageable.

Think about talking to a financial advisor about what your money goals are. You say, "I want to save a million dollars before I retire." They put your age, your income, and your retirement age into their fancy calculator and tell you roughly how much you need to save per month to get there. You start with that first month of saving, or even that first week. Yeah, she looks small now, but just wait until you see her in thirty years! Or even next year! She is going to be beautiful! **Consistency x time = results.**

Do you know what a great by-product of consistency is? You have likely built a fantastic **habit**. Congratulations! By forcing yourself in the beginning and holding yourself accountable in the long run, you have built a habit, whether this is a great work ethic, being physically active, action toward a passion, or a side hustle. Consistency rarely has a negative side effect in the goal crushing arena. You have proven to yourself you can do something challenging.

That said, all of that 80/20 talk applies here too. We are humans. There are times we are going to skip, but in the beginning, especially in the middle of a mental battle with yourself, it had better be for a good reason!

That is where mindset vs. channel capacity comes in. *Can* you do it, but you just don't want to? Or is it a, "I worked my fourth twelve-hour shift yesterday which was four of five and I truly just need to mentally and physically rest instead of waking up early to get to the gym" kind of thing?

Again, as an adult, nobody else holding you accountable in those facets of your life. Only *you* can make these decisions and you know when you really need it or when you are just being lazy. Can you be lazy sometimes? You sure can – right after you put thirty minutes into this important goal you have set for yourself. But hey, this is coming from the mom of three with multiple jobs who gives herself a lot of grace. I hold myself accountable most days and there are days I just don't get it done – but I run through the same self-checking first. And you know what? Sometimes I am being lazy, I know it, and I still don't get it done. I try to keep those days to a minimum, but sometimes they are just needed.

Overall, if you are following that 80/20 rule, you should be in good shape. But heed this warning. The more you skip in the beginning, the less likely you are to succeed. Remember, consistency can sometimes feel like a snail moving forward, but hey, it's moving!

Dig deep and use what you have...

Where are my fellow college athletes? I know you remember all of that practice, training, and conditioning. Understand this, you have *years* of physical and mental training just waiting to be reactivated in a different way.

Back in the day when I played volleyball and was running on the treadmill, some days I wanted to quit early. My mental trick was that I would make myself run for "one more song". And then one more. And then one more. I would get to my goal one song at a time. Or envisioning my team winning the game as I stood ready to serve the ball with the game on the line and my heart pounding in my chest. Eyes closed, deep breath. You got this.

I use some of the mental pep talks that I used to give myself now in my professional life when I have to be confident despite being nervous, or whatever the situation might call for.

What about my cancer fighters? Now I *know* you can handle *whatever* comes your way and I know you do as well.

I am truly amazed by the friends that I have seen go through this and how much they have juggled and overcome. Did life get put on pause until their treatment was over? Did they get to take a year off work until they were feeling up to the task again? Um, no. Their babies still needed to eat (three times a day no less). They still needed to pay their bills. Laundry needed to be done. The dog was still leaving hair all over the house.

They thought their cup was already full and then they received a cancer diagnosis. They had no choice, but to cram a whole bunch more into that cup and just *make* it happen. If you had that resolve then, you can find it again. ❤My hat is off to every person going through that or supporting someone they love who is. May you get back to health soon and feel surrounded by the love of your village on your journey. ❤

Speaking of villages - another thing to remember is that you do not have to do this alone! Oh, on the contrary! You can load up on all the help you need – just make sure it's the *right* help. Don't go calling your bestie who hates doing whatever it is you are trying to do or does not support this journey of yours, as it will ultimately lead to you leaving her in that ER by herself – no, no, no. You need to have people who are going to give you the, "Get up and get it done" that you are looking for.

Let me give you an example of the wrong type of support for your issue. I have a group of friends who I met on my first nursing unit many years ago and we still hang out to this day. **Love them to death.** Although they are the best in so many ways, they have been less than enthusiastic when it comes to my progress on this book. For example, I would send a group text asking what they thought of an idea for my title, and two days later I might get a 'like' from one of them.

"Hey! Does anybody want to read my first chapter?" – crickets.

These have been my friends for close to **twenty years**, albeit *not* the right friends for help with this book. Sound familiar?

On the flip side, when I signed up to run that marathon, one of the factors that I took into account was that my girlfriend Nicole (one of the friends I just mentioned above) had already signed up. She is one of the smartest nurses I know and a total beast when it comes to fitness. Back in the day she was hitting the gym twice a day and has *zero* room for your bullshit excuses. I was as good as crossing that finish line because she was *not* skipping a long run, and *I would* be getting into that car when she came to pick me up.

Find your Nicole. You may have a different one for different goals, you may have a few – whatever works, but an accountability partner or like-minded, motivated people surrounding you exponentially increases your chances of success and may serve to make the whole process a lot more fun.

There are also times the universe just knows what you need and positively delivers! I mentioned at the beginning of this book that I reached out to Dr. Jason Selk, author of *Organize Tomorrow Today* and his response not only motivated me but has been in the back of my mind as I hold myself accountable as well.

Dr. Selk, if you ever read this, I can't thank you enough for being so incredibly awesome.

> **Morning Liz, CONGRATS on your success, you should be VERY proud of the effort you are putting into making people better.**
>   **WE NEED MORE LIKE YOU IN THIS WORLD.**
>   **Yes of course you can use my materials, anything that helps you better serve others is a WIN FOR ALL OF US.**
>   **If you liked OTT, I highly recommend my latest book RELENTLESS SOLUTION FOCUS, many have said it's my best work yet. Might make a nice Christmas gift for that friend that turned you on to OTT.**
>   **KEEP ATTACKING.**
>   **Dr. Jason Selk**

I mean after reading that and screaming like a high-school teenager how could I *not* go forward and conquer?! It was such a huge motivator and I am quite sure he has no clue just what an impact that small gesture made on me and my hope is to motivate just one other person through this book to get up and reach their own goals.

I can't...

These two words get in the way of accountability all the time. I want to, but I can't. Let's dive into this short phrase for a bit as you may find that if you replaced the words "I can't" with "I won't," or "I don't want to" it is likely more accurate. Let's try a few examples:

I would like to go back to school but I can't afford it.	I would like to go back to school, but I don't want to take a loan/figure out the budget- or work overtime to help pay for it.
I want to go back to school, but I don't have any time to work that overtime.	I want to go back to school, but I am not open-minded to the fact that OT at my current job is not the only way to make extra money.
I want to get into leadership, but I can't work five days a week.	I want to be a leader, but I won't work five days a week if it takes away from other things I enjoy.
No, I can't work five days a week - I have kids!	I have three kids and I get it. It may seem like the most complicated puzzle in history and cost money, but at the end of the day, you likely CAN figure it out.

As you can see, can't sets our brains up to sell ourselves short and essentially fail before we even start. You *can* do most things but start by asking yourself if you WANT to do them. If you truly do, the timing may not be right to put in the effort and hustle required. Or are you waiting for the perfect time and passing up the right time? For example, I *could* go back to school to get my Doctorate in Nursing (DNP). It would take a whole bunch of work, but not one cell in my body is interested in doing that at this time, so I will not be putting any effort into this. This is very different from saying "I can't," so let's start replacing that word with more accurate and appropriate ones. This is another mindset shift issue that then bleeds into accountability as we are not going to hold ourselves accountable for something we have convinced ourselves we cannot do before even trying. If you find yourself saying the word "can't" more often than not, it's time for a shift.

I just don't feel like it...

There may be times when you know you can do something, but you just don't feel like it. Something that I have found incredibly useful in these situations is the combination of a goal and a plan. These do not have to be super complicated and sometimes they are very obvious, such as completing coursework for a degree or training for a marathon.

However, let's say I want to get into better shape. It's early in the morning and it's a beautiful day outside. I *could* run right now, but I am not feeling particularly motivated to do so. The alternative is sitting out on the deck drinking coffee in peace and quiet. That sounds *lovely*. *This* is where a plan/goal comes in handy. The goal of "I want to get into better shape", is simply not specific enough. What does that even mean?

That could incorporate cardio, weights, diet – all of it...or none of it. On the other hand, if you say, "I want to lift weights two to three times a week and run twice a week," that is *much* more specific and therefore much more actionable. If that were my goal, I would look at what day it was (Friday) and ask myself, "Where am I on this goal?" I would then tell myself that I have lifted weights twice this week and gone running once.

Then, I would look at the rest of my week and make a plan of action. Now I can see that this is a perfect opportunity to meet my goal and that I should seize the moment where I actually feel like running and afterward, I can feel very accomplished going into my weekend knowing I have met my workout goal for the week.

Having a plan is similar to having a prescription for success – it is hard to hold yourself accountable when you do not have anything very specific to hold yourself accountable to or for.

Make a plan, write it down, and make it happen.

[EE2]Created by Gan Khoon Lay from the Noun Project www.thenoun-project.com [EE3]www.coffeeandmotivation.com

Chapter 5

Self-reflection – figuring out your 'why'

"Find your why and you will find your way."
−John C. Maxwell

Key Points & Takeaways:

- What is your current relationship with your job? Are you in love? Casual dating? On the rocks?
- Self-check-ins should be a regular part of your mental wellness. Be intentional and schedule them if you need to.
- Create times your brain can wander. This could be while driving, running, having morning coffee, etc.
- Ask yourself what you want. (Then watch The Notebook with Ryan Gosling) What you want can and will likely change over time.
- Make a list of what bothers you and brainstorm possible solutions.

Self-reflection is the star of the show. As you can see on the pyramid, it's written in sparkly gold. If this book is not printed in color, please use your imagination, and know that she is sparkly and beautiful!

CHAPTER 5

Self-reflection can be summarized by many things: checking in with yourself, being in tune with yourself, listening to your gut. Some people do this often, some call it prayer, and some may claim they have never done it because they are too busy worrying about everyone else or have no clue where to start.

©2022 Straight Talk, RN LLC

No matter where you fall on that continuum, I cannot stress enough that it's incredibly important to reflect regularly. "Regular" can be different for every person and can also vary for the same person throughout their lives, but in essence, self-reflection is our personal nursing plan of care – our guide. The forces or signals that are guiding us in our decision-making throughout our lives. For many people, self-reflection happens naturally during times of change. For example, you need to move because you have a growing family. Where to go? Or maybe you are close to finishing school and are wondering what you want to do (if anything yet) with your new degree.

Holidays are natural times for many to check in with themselves or reflect. We tend to reflect on our lives, our friends, and our family and hopefully feel grateful for what we have and the people we love in our lives past and present. Although this is wonderful, ideally, we are also self-reflecting more often than just around the holidays to ensure that we continue to move forward in the right direction.

But what about doing this for your career? How do you even do this?

Exercise – evaluate your current job

Let's start by getting a mental handle on our current situation. If you can, jot down a few thoughts on a piece of paper or a notes app on your phone.

Ask yourself what your current relationship with your job is like.

- Happily married?
- Looking to see other people and keep it casual?
- Maybe it's been on the rocks for a while?

Now, ask yourself how you feel while you are working most of the time.

Not sure?

CHAPTER 5

Try this: Go to work and write down how you feel during different times of the day.

- What is making you smile/laugh?
- What is triggering your frustrations?
- When are you feeling short-tempered or annoyed?
- Are you bored?
- Do you feel like you are swimming through your day with ease?

You can start a little workday journal, like a food journal. Focus on what you like and don't like about your job.

Jot down thoughts and feelings before, during and after a shift.

Even if you are not able to write anything, simply paying attention to this is a great start. At the end of the day review what you wrote/how you felt. Was it overall more positive, more negative, or mixed?

Hopefully, even if you are currently unhappy in your job, you may be able to look at some of your notes and see parts of your job that stand out and make you happy. Is there a way to incorporate more of what makes you happy into your current job? Less of what makes you unhappy?

Doing small exercises like this can also help us to gain greater clarity on your 'why':

- Why do we go to work?
- What do we hope to internally accomplish?
- What feeds our soul?

This is also great information to serve as our guiding light when it comes to our careers over the years as we figure out what is next.

Use your people...

I have a lot of aunts and uncles. My dad is one of nine kids, and my mom is one of seven. One of my aunts once described herself as an 'external processor' meaning she processed things by talking about them out loud with others. This is extremely common and can very much be a part of self-reflection. All of my Ted Lasso fans out there, you may have some form of the "Diamond Dogs" in your life for dating or marriage troubles, or perhaps you talk to your parents or siblings. They might also be great to talk to about what you want to do with your life professionally. They are the people that know you very well and can give insight into some of your strengths and where you might use them.

On the other hand, sometimes family advice doesn't work for various reasons and it may be best to leave your personal and professional groups separate. I would suggest at least one person you know fairly well. A trusted co-worker perhaps? Ideally, it will be someone who is going to be honest with you and can give you constructive feedback when needed. You do not want a bunch of ego stroking or enabling; you need someone who is going to be supportive but shoot you straight.

If you know what career path you want to take and can find someone who is several steps ahead of you, they might also be a great addition to your support system as they can tell you what worked and didn't work along the way and offer valuable real-life advice.

Perhaps you are lucky enough to have a mentor in your life – a sage individual that you feel you can turn to for advice about anything under the sun? That's a great place to start and I suggest you check in with them at least a couple of times a year at minimum.

I never self-reflect. I think it is stupid, I don't have time, blah, blah, blah...

Okay. Hello! We have some work to do but don't worry, you will see that it's pretty simple. First and foremost, we are going to have to be intentional about setting a goal to do this. I have a feeling that when we start to do this, you will likely realize that you already self-reflect on some level, but just didn't recognize it as such.

Step 1: Think about a time or activity where your mind can wander. This can be before bed, (but just make sure you are still getting enough sleep!) on your commute, (in my opinion, is the *ideal* time), or a walk with the dog. You can also zone out during an activity where your brain does not have to be actively engaged such as folding laundry, doing the dishes, etc. In order to turn this into a habit, we want to find an activity that you do fairly often so you can practice this thinking regularly.

For example, Sara Blakely talked about how she did her best thinking while she was driving. She lived about six minutes from her office at Spanx, but she would drive an hour to work just to allow herself time for her mind to wander and to possibly be inspired by her next great idea.

Step 2: The next time you are doing the activity picked in Step 1, ask yourself some of the questions that we just went over in the previous work exercise, where we pay attention to how we feel throughout the day. I have a few bonus ones below:

- What would I change about my job if I could?

- **What future opportunities do I have there, and am I interested in any of those?**
- What about my peers? Do I like them?
- Am I happy where I am, or do I feel it is time for a change?

Step 3: Keep moving. Obviously, there are a million questions that you may ask yourself. If it turns out all of your answers are positive and you feel as though it is not time for a change, great! Hopefully, at the very least, you have identified the specifics of *why* you like your current job and feel reinvigorated that you are in the right place. If this is the case, it is time to set a few small goals which we will work on in the next chapter. Having work goals, even small ones, keeps you mentally moving forward so that you're less likely to feel stuck in a rut. Which goals to set have a lot to do with where you want to end up, and self-reflection helps to shed some light on where that might be.

Something else that keeps us moving is a sense of purpose or your 'why'. Sara Blakely defined this in a way that really resonated with me. She said people used to ask her what her purpose was, and it would completely freak her out. Simply put (which is another reason I love it) she says she thought about her purpose as an intersection between what brings her joy, what she is good at, and how she wants to serve the world.

CHAPTER 5

[1]

Where those three intersect is ideally where you concentrate your time and effort. They say where you invest your love, you invest your life. We do not have limitless resources in terms of our time, energy, or attention, so investing them in places that matter is important!

This framework is derived from the Japanese concept of Ikigai [EE4] which is similar to the French term "reason for being". A quick internet search of "Ikigai" will bring up many venn diagrams and articles you can read to help you to gain clarity on your own why. There are also great books written on the topic such as *"Start with Why"* by Simon Sinek. A good friend of mine recommended his book to me when I called him as part of my own self-reflection and I recommend it to anyone who is trying to figure out their own direction forward.

One nurse's hell is another's paradise – find *your* peace...

Here is what I think is amazing: there is a spot for all of us. Seriously. Think about it. There are nurses like me who love the ER and nurses that get mental hives at the mere thought of having to be involved in a multi-victim-trauma resuscitation. On the flip side, some nurses want to help patients die peacefully while others just want to hold babies. Great news—you are all hired! The more you can find people, activities, and passions that feed your soul, the better off you will be. Try lots of things and take note of what makes you smile and what makes you cringe.

Beware of social media...

I can't talk about self-reflection without talking about social media. So many people see someone they want to be based on what they post (typically high income, beautiful home, lots of travel). They hardly consider the years of everyday work that is required to get there, what the other ninety-nine percent of their life looks like outside their social media posts, or that it may not even be real in the first place. We all know that for the most part, only the bright and shiny stuff is posted on social media—not all of the trial and error, misses, work, and less glamorous stuff. You have likely done this yourself! You go on a trip and you post the ten coolest shots, not the other 165 "eh" ones.

Don't put all of your time and effort into achieving a goal simply because someone else is doing it. You will likely be way less happy than you thought and wish you had not wasted all of this time and energy getting there. You'll find yourself saying, "This grass doesn't look so green now that I'm standing right on top of it. I miss my old grass."

The silver lining is that you will have learned a huge lesson: that this isn't what you truly want. Let's take that knowledge and move on to our next goal.

One final PSA (Public Service Announcement) I think is so very important regarding social media: *everything* is relative, and the only true judge is you. Let's think about our global world for a minute.

There are likely *thousands* of people who would look at your current life on paper or your social media reel and think about how much they would love to trade places with you. *You* are likely one of the people that many others would see as a goal. You might have your nursing license for one – that is a big goal to lots of aspiring nurses out there. Remember that! Recognize how far you have come and be grateful for what you currently have.

Your quest for the next thing should be fueled by real substance, such as your 'why,' or a personal challenge of some sort, instead of reaching for a shiny object for no reason other than status. Don't take my word for it, but the chances are pretty great that if the road to that endpoint was not one filled with personal meaning and fulfillment, the destination may feel pretty shallow and empty once you get there. You hear about folks that have made so much money but are still unhappy all the time. Sure, there are people out there where money *is* their only driving factor and hey —I'm not here to judge. If making the most money possible is why you wake up every morning *and* that makes you truly happy, then get out there and slay. What if you could make those dollars *while* doing something that feeds your soul?! *That* is my unicorn right there.

You know you best. Trust your gut and be true to your soul.

[1] From Sara Blakely Masterclass www.masterclass.com

[EE4]https://positivepsychology.com/ikigai/
   Adapted from positivephyscholoy.com's toolkit 2020

Chapter 6

Goals – Let's set a few

"A goal without a plan is only a dream."
– Brian Tracy

Key Points & Takeaways:

- Goals should be actionable and attainable, but this does not necessarily mean easy.
- Give yourself a due date for extra credit.
- Ideally, pick one goal at a time to focus on, otherwise your efforts may be spread too thin.
- Your goals are personal – don't waste your time trying to achieve other people's goals.

Adults are always asking kids what they want to be when they grow up. Chances are you may have asked a child this yourself. It's likely that when you were young, you had goals about the big things – whether or not you wanted to go to college, get married, have kids, and what you wanted to do for your career, among others. For example, I told myself that by the time I was thirty, I wanted to be married, have a child, and finish my master's degree. I also had a goal of becoming a manager or some sort of leader as my advanced degree was in nursing administration. I felt very accomplished when I had achieved my goals by my due date with four months to spare.

Many years and jobs later, I had my name outside my office door as a manager at the number one hospital in the state, and I was so incredibly proud of myself. It had taken a lot of work to get there and I had arrived. But, as you will likely guess, the story does not end there. In fact, in a way, it began when I had finally reached the last big career goal that I had set for myself at the time...

CHAPTER 6

I loved my team and felt like I was making a difference in the department in small ways that mattered to me. I was working with my long-time work family and had the best co-manager possible (much love, Red). Life was crazy busy but great.

Then I had my third child while I was the manager, and when I went to work, she was still asleep. When I got home, she was already in bed for the night. Rinse and repeat.

I started to feel like I was missing everything at home and that there was nothing that I could do about it. I mean, it was a busy, 24/7, level-one trauma center. My hours were all over the place. Late nights, early mornings, but whatever they were, they tended to be long because my commute was tacked on to every one of them. My commute from door to desk was about an hour and a half each way. That is three hours every day commuting to work. WOOF.

I tried taking the train sometimes, and although it helped mentally, it didn't help me save much time. Have you ever missed a train by mere moments? It's so frustrating. Not to mention, once I got off the train, I had to take a shuttle bus the rest of the way. In short, it was a grind, and over time, it started to catch up with me.

So, there I was without much direction since I had met all of my professional goals. I realized at that time that I had failed to set any new ones. I had the loud and clear signal that I needed to make a change, but I was finally in *the job* that I had thought about for close to ten years! The entire reason why I went back to school in the first place!

Mentally, I felt stuck and had no clue which way I was facing. I was never home. During the week, I missed everything. No dinners at home, no sporting events, maybe bedtime for my older ones once or twice a week. I realized that even if I worked hard to get promoted, the schedule might be better, but the hospital would not be one inch closer. It was non-negotiable. That commute was not going anywhere. What is a girl to do?

First, I had to make the hugely significant decision to choose my family as my why and guiding factor. That was step one and a big internal battle. I set a goal to find a better balance and then I worked backward one step at a time.

I took my director out for a beer and told her how I was feeling, even though I had *no clue* what my next job was going to be at the time. This is not the method I would recommend for most sane people, but I was crazy lucky in that I *knew* Heather would support me through this. She could not have been more amazing. She listened and then said that I would never get those years back and that I would always regret it if I didn't make a change. She even offered to help me figure out what was next.

So, great question—what *was* next?! Here's the thing about saying stuff out loud to other people (especially to your BOSS): once it's out there, there is no going back. The horse had left the barn. It was time for me to figure out what I was going to do with my life, and quickly, as I had essentially just quit my job without having another one lined up. YIKES.

I started with what I knew and felt comfortable with—conversations. I picked five different people in five different areas that I was potentially interested in to talk to. Education, operations, consulting, entrepreneurship, and my HR (human resources) partner at the hospital. Jackie, our HR partner, was someone whom I respected. She had a great overarching view of what roles were available at the company and was also a working mom. How did I find these people, you may ask? Many of them were people I had worked with, and two of them were warm introductions made through colleagues. Using what resources I had, I asked specific questions, and this small network was able to suggest people to speak to and help me arrange meetings and other details in the process. I reached out to all of them and asked for thirty minutes of their time. It was super helpful for me to talk things out with multiple people who had unique dispositions and questions for me to consider.

One thing led to another, and I ended up moving into a work-from-home job. And the best part? They let me go back per diem and work as a staff nurse in the ER. I have been going back to work on weekends ever since and I truly could not be happier with the mix. I get to see all of my people, have my twelve hours of crazy, and then say, "Peace out! See you in a week or two." It was exactly what I needed and I will be forever grateful to everyone who took the time to help me sort all this out. It was definitely a stressful time in my life, but it worked out beautifully and I am so much happier in my current spot.

Goals need to be real.

Goals can be lofty, but to achieve them, you need to either put in the work needed or adjust them. Let me share a real example to highlight what I mean.

My girlfriend Chelsea wants it all, and she is *not* willing to compromise. She wants more money, no weekends or holidays, no twelves, and total control over her schedule so that she can spend time with her kids and take them to their sports. Preach, girl! Same! There is no reason why she cannot have this.

The issue? She wants all of these in her next job – and has a list of things that she does not want to do in order to achieve this goal. She does not have an advanced degree, is not certified in her specialty (which holds you back at my hospital), does not want to go into a five-days-a-week leadership position, refuses to take a job where she cannot take her girls to school in the morning, and is also unwilling to take a lateral move or pay cut in any way. Oh, and she holds the insurance and doesn't want to change that either. You may be saying to yourself, "And she shouldn't!"

While I do not disagree with you, hear me out.

I worry Chelsea may be short-sighted here, and I have told her this more times than I can count as I love her and want her to succeed. What I'm trying to get her to see is that although her next job may not check all her boxes (because let's face it, she has *a lot* of them to check), it may open the door to a job eventually that does. For example, when I took my ER manager job, it was my first five-days-a-week job. I liked it, but commuting so much into the city was the death of me. However, that leadership experience opened tons of doors for me in terms of opportunity, and that has been the message I have been trying to pound into her head with little success. Girl works HARD. My wish is that she would put some of that hard work and hustle into something that sets herself up to make more and work less in the long run.

Your next job may not be 'the job,' but it might be the door to it.

Don't get me wrong—I am *all for* the dream job mentality, but if you are sitting around complaining about your current job and not doing the work it takes to grab that next job, we have an issue. It's like waiting around to win the lottery instead of saving for retirement. Sure, it totally could happen, but in the meantime, while we wait, I suggest we take some accountability and action.

Chances are, even if you are happy with where you are right now, there may be opportunities in your current role that you have yet to explore or capitalize on. Examples may include leadership opportunities, such as being a preceptor, a charge nurse, etc. However, it's likely there are smaller ones as well, such as a project, a committee role, or a department change. Perhaps the exercise in the last chapter has highlighted one or two opportunities in your job that you're interested in. If not, dig them out. That way, you have goals to keep in mind whenever you feel the itch to shake things up a bit. Any time you feel dissatisfied, you can choose to take a step on the path towards your next goal.

Your goals should be just that – *your* goals...

I have always been very career driven. I went back to school only a year after becoming a nurse because I knew I wanted to be in leadership someday and wanted to "get it done."

After I had my children, the working parent "juggle" became very real. The number of things that need to be coordinated was just crazy. It *can* be done, but it sometimes feels like balancing a two-ton weight on a pinpoint—the margin for error feels very tiny. Not to mention, you feel like you are constantly hustling to ensure that all the bases are covered and none of the balls are dropping.

When I decided to walk away from healthcare leadership, the two parts of my life that I had worked very hard at were seemingly at complete odds, and it seemed so unfair. After fifteen years of working towards a goal, I was now choosing to walk away from the ladder. It felt very incompatible with my old pre-children self and that feeling sat in my gut for a while.

Cue the universe.

Catching up with nurses that I know and have worked with over the years is one of my favorite things to do. After nearly twenty years and with the way people come and go in that ER, you can imagine that I have worked with literally *hundreds* of nurses.

Not too long ago, I caught up with a friend of mine who came to our ER as a student. We called Justin 'TMF' for "too much fun" and loved him from day one. Many years later, everyone agrees that TMF is killing it. He is a trauma coordinator at the premiere hospital for trauma and just graduated with his advanced degree with a plan to go into academia. He also continues teaching trauma education, at which he is fantastic. He has had so many cool opportunities to travel and meet amazing people in the crazy world of trauma medicine.

One of the things that he said to me as we were talking was that he had no interest or intention of ever moving any higher than his current role. "I'm happy where I am. I don't want to move any farther away from the patients and the nurses," he said. I have heard this many times through the years and truly believe it in my soul yet needed to be reminded of it at that moment. Just because you have a twenty-foot ladder does not mean you need to climb all twenty feet to the top rung. Climb to where you are happy and stay there until you are not. Then, when your arm starts to hurt or you are unhappy, move up or find a new ladder. Stop worrying about what everyone else thinks you *should* do and do what you *want* to do.

CHAPTER 6

This is it. Your only life. Do what *you* want with it.

You've met your goals. Now what?

Perhaps you are like me in that you have met all your goals and realize that you have yet to set any new ones, or so much as to even *think* about professional goals in quite some time. Often as we get older, we typically set fewer professional goals for a variety of reasons. We may set fewer big life goals altogether once we knock off the ones we had when we were younger, like buying a house, getting married, or having kids. Those are all such *huge* accomplishments, and it feels so good to cross them off the list.

One thing I want to point out is that we don't always need to be swinging for the fences when we create our goals. Smaller goals can serve multiple purposes. We have already discussed how they can serve to keep you motivated on your way to larger ones. They can also serve as a backup plan of sorts in the event your first plan doesn't work out the way you thought it would, or they can simply be ways that you challenge yourself and grow alongside your current job.

Perhaps your self-reflection told you that you currently really like your job, but you are ready for a challenge. Is that available in your current job? Or maybe it is time for a side hustle? Maybe you do not need a new job at all, but a second source of income? Ideally, a side hustle would be something that balances out your primary job, something less stressful, with a better schedule, or even more fun. It's great if it can be something that becomes your primary job, but it doesn't have to be.

Example 1 - side hustle: I did home infusions for a while. It was great money, and I even got paid for mileage! I would go to my patient's house and start their IV, give them their medication, and sit there and monitor them like you would a blood transfusion. Many times, they would fall asleep during the infusion, so I was left to do whatever I needed to do in between assessments. This could be schoolwork, reading, planning your week, doing your finances, writing a book—whatever you want! Was it easy? *So easy.* Good money? Absolutely, especially considering how easy it was. Good schedule? Definitely, since I could set it myself. Could it become my primary job? Not a chance. While it was a perfect side hustle, I would have been bored to tears if it was the only thing I was doing.

Example 2 – this book: I have always thought about writing a book. Initially, I wasn't sure what I would write about. I would ask myself, "What am I passionate enough to write a book about?" or "What would people (aside from my immediate family who are required to read any book I write) want to read about?" It wasn't until last year when I was walking with my neighbor bestie for the hundredth time talking about what was next for me when I had an 'aha' moment where all the stars aligned, and I realized I did NOT need a new job to cure my restless soul. Instead, I realized that I needed to follow my passion in a creative way all on my own. That is when I started my own business – Straight Talk, RN LLC (https://straighttalkrn.com/). My passion has always been for career coaching, advice and motivation for nurses, so I finally had a book topic.

We now had step one, but then what? I have never written a book, I'm not in that world even a tiny bit, so the whole process seemed very overwhelming. Thinking about writing a book and the actual process of writing and publishing a book are very different issues.

Cue the universe.

CHAPTER 6

Earlier this year, my very young and healthy cousin was diagnosed with a kind of sarcoma cancer that he has no business having. Our entire family was devastated to say the least. While I am confident that he will beat it, I couldn't help to reflect on life and about what he would say to me if he and I were walking around the block instead. As a former life coach himself, I knew he would say, "Liz, this life as we know it is not promised. Look at me and this crazy cancer diagnosis that I never saw coming. You want to do something? Then do it already. Stop wasting time."

After all, who knows this better than those the medical field? I have seen so much in the ER over the last twenty years. The good, the bad, and the ugly. People who were not supposed to die or get those terrible scan results that changed their lives forever in an instant. I knew he was right.

I came across a program on my Instagram feed for writing books, listened to the pitch, sized up the work and the cost, and threw my hat in the ring. I put my money where my mouth was, put on my big girl pants, and decided to just go for it. And here I am! As of this moment, I am 15,000 words into this journey and hope to have this book published by the end of summer. Trust me when I say this: if I can do this, anyone who truly wants to can as well. I have three busy kids, two and a half jobs, and a whole lot of laundry.

I would say that one of the biggest things I have learned is to not be so hung up on how you are getting there—just take a step forward.

Because here's the thing about goals—we set these all the time! It's called a checklist. We have things that we want to get done, we write them down, and we get them done. Boom. See? Not so hard. All checks are wins, but consistency is what will truly move the dial towards your larger goal. This is why being intentional becomes so important. Small goals can build upon one another as a way to achieve a larger goal. Write them down. This simple step increases your chances of success in leaps and bounds. It's like a mini contract with yourself. It is easy to ignore, and easy to put off things that either seem big and daunting or those that do not bring us immediate joy. For many of you, career planning and goal setting fits squarely into *both* of those categories.

The key is this: Set *specific* and *actionable* goals. What does that mean? If you read the accountability chapter, I gave an example of this where instead of saying, "I want to get into shape," say, "I want to lift weights two-three times a week and run twice a week." The second goal is much more specific and therefore more actionable. It's clear what needs to be done to achieve this goal.

That brings up the next big topic around goals – your **due date.**

Ooh-wee! Stuff just got real. Not only did we set a specific goal, but we wrote it down *and* the date by which we wanted to accomplish it. Those two things—writing it down and assigning a due date —just made you *way* more likely to accomplish that goal. It costs you zero dollars and maybe thirty seconds of your time. Let's think about this for a quick minute. "I want to run a marathon" vs. "I want to run a marathon by the time I am thirty years old." The second one is way more actionable since you now know when you have to get your butt in gear to accomplish this. Once you have a goal and a target date, you can get to work by identifying the steps that will get you there on time.

Example 3– going back to school: Let's say you want to be an acute care nurse practitioner (NP) in the next three to five years. Your next steps are to gather information and choose a program that fits your needs (cost, online vs. in person, etc.). Talk to NPs that you know or friends that may be able to introduce you to some NPs. Ask them about school and the programs they were in. Get an idea of what you are getting yourself into in terms of time, cost, etc. If your goal is in three-five years, then pick a program that works best for your timeline and goals and get going! Don't overanalyze.

I have goals for days. Look out world!

Maybe you already have all the goals. You are trying to do it all as fast as possible. First, I love your motivation and energy! To increase your success in any of these goals, though, you need to prioritize them. Your time is like your money; it is a finite resource. You need to be purposeful about where you use and spend your time, since there are lots of unimportant tasks that likely take up all of your minutes. Like social media. Woof – what a rabbit hole of wasted hours. Skiiiiip – you have stuff to do. That being said, don't try to do too many things at once, like trying to cook scrambled eggs while curling your hair and replying to a work email all at the same time. I promise you, *one* of those things, if not all, will likely turn out poorly.

Pick one. For example, right now I have prioritized getting this book written. My mind is focused on this task. I might get an idea for a social media post here and there, but I do not want to get distracted, because writing a book demands all of my extra time and attention. If I am meeting my word count and find that I still have time, I can either continue to write or maybe post some content, work on my email list, etc., but only after I have met my primary goal.

I have to remind myself of this often.

After all, scrolling through social media can make you instantly feel like you are not doing enough. Or that you are not doing the "right" things. You may start to second guess yourself or feel like you need to be creating content that does not line up with your priorities or your style because everyone else seems to be doing it. You kill yourself to create all this content that you don't particularly like that is fairly meaningless to you because the pressure to do "something" felt so overwhelming. Meanwhile, you have three kids, a husband, and a dog, its baseball season, and dinners need to be made...

You get the idea. Life can be a lot.

This is when I remind myself that I need to control my day and not let my day control me. I go back to what I learned in *Organize Tomorrow Today* and regroup. I remind myself that I do not have to get everything done. I simply need to get the most important things done. There is a big difference.

So, what is my current goal? I must say, it's a big one. You may think I am talking about writing a book, but really that is just the first step. I talk more about it in the, "What's next..." section at the end of the book, but I would like to grow my company over the years to eventually take over my 9-5. To be in complete control of *when* and *where* I work. Not to mention, doing something that truly feeds my soul. Career coaching for nurses, speaking to large groups of nurses all over the country. This book is just one of the seeds I am planting to see how they grow over the next decade or so. I have no idea what will happen over the next ten years and that is okay.

What I do know is that I am following a passion, listening to my internal compass, and am willing to take some chances and see where the road

CHAPTER 6

takes me. The fact that I do not know exactly what will happen next is part of the adventure.

Chapter 7

Action – nursing is a target that moves with you

"Well done is better than well said."
- Benjamin Franklin

Key Points & Takeaways:

- You have to *do* something. Thinking about it gets you nowhere.
- Many opportunities are passed by as they look like plain old work.
- Networking is connecting with like-minded people, not selling used cars.
- Don't underestimate small, consistent actions. Be patient.
- Think about the impressions you make on others. If it's not the one you want to leave, own it, and change it.
- It's okay to change your mind and pivot. Don't waste your time on things that do not bring you joy.

Next year will mark my twentieth year as a nurse, and for someone who got into the field at the very last minute on an educated whim, I have to say, the longer I'm in the field the more I appreciate it.

CHAPTER 7

I look at my husband and twin sister, both teachers, and they have done the same job for twenty years with minimal variation. They have limited options for true change outside of becoming an administrator or guidance counselor. Every day they are in front of students teaching them something. I cannot waste this opportunity to give a shout-out to all the teachers out there. In many ways, they are the nurses of the education field: incredibly essential, yet often overworked, underpaid, and feeling underappreciated.

That said, in terms of variations, nursing is the exact opposite. I could write a list of all the different areas nurses can work in, and I promise you I would miss close to a hundred possibilities. (I plan to keep a list on my website- if you have some to add email them to me!) The crazy thing about having limitless options is that it can also be a bit of a double-edged sword at times. There you stand in the grocery store aisle with countless boxes of cereal. You need to choose. What do you feel like having? So. Many. Options.

The question I want to throw on the table is, "Who said you had to just pick one?" Have you ever known those people that mix two kinds of cereal at the same time? Talk about crazy. This may or may not be the case when it comes to work, too. As I mentioned earlier on in this book, I had four different jobs for four years, and it was such a perfect fit for me at the time. I worked per diem in the ER, and I worked sixteen-hours a week as a nurse educator teaching third-year medical students skills such as foley insertion and IV starts during their surgical clerkship. I also had several patients whom I would see for intravenous immunoglobulin (IVIG) home infusions, and I worked as a nurse for the Chicago Cubs at Wrigley Field in the First Aid Office (Hi, Peach!). Of course, none of these were full-time—so much fun though. Plus, I never felt like I had to choose just one.

Perhaps you have interviewed for two jobs that are both listed as full-time. During the interview process, why not ask if there is any flexibility in the hours? For example, one of my nursing friends was able to negotiate four ten-hour days instead of five eight-hour days for a quality-control job she accepted. The worst they can say is no, right?

Another thing you should always ask for is for better pay! When I interviewed for my medical school job, we discussed salary. As a nurse, I had never been asked and I completely low balled myself. I told them meekly, "Well, I would like to make at least what I am making now in the ER," and thankfully they ignored me, as they paid a full ten dollars an hour *more* than I made in the ER. And it was *fun* with zero stress! What?! Jobs like that actually *exist*?! Game changer.

Several years later, a surgeon that I used to work with asked if I would come to a different hospital to run his clinic. The dynamic woman who hired me at the medical school told me something that stuck with me ever since. She told me that when someone tells you about an opportunity, your answer should always be, "Tell me more." So, even though I wasn't actively looking for a new job at the time, that is what I said.

I ended up going out there for a day to interview and shadow the position. When I sat down with the director, she told me what the salary range was. I countered with a number about twenty percent higher and said it was the lowest I could go. To my surprise, she didn't bat an eye, telling me she would see what she could do. On my drive home, they called and said they could offer me what I asked for.

Nurses – negotiate! Do your salary homework and ask for more. Again, the worst they can say is no.

CHAPTER 7

For the sake of argument, let's say you *have* to pick one job only. How do you choose? First, consider **where** you are right now. Are you going to be a new nurse practitioner, or is this a move to a new state and you are going to be the new kid on the block? Have you been doing this for ten years, maybe twenty? Next, find the **'why'** behind your move. Are you looking for less stress? Do you miss being at your kid's sporting events on the weekend? That 'why' should be your leading decision-maker in your next adventure. Seems simple, right?

My advice to you is, as early on in the process as possible, while you are in tune with your gut and the universe and the 'why' for change is fresh, *write this down*. Notes section of your phone, a few words – done. As you are searching and interviewing, there is a good possibility you will be overwhelmed and maxed out in terms of channel capacity and the decision will only become muddier and more complicated. You may even get swayed by no weekends or holidays, or more money and come to find that you are still unhappy in the end because what was *actually* important to you had not changed for the better.

In my experience, when we do not lead with our 'why,' and our priorities when it comes to a new job, it likely will not take long for the new to wear off and for us to realize we are just as unhappy as we were before. On the flip side, maybe the 'no weekends' *was* all you needed and you feel pretty satisfied. Who knows – it could go either way. And there you have it – it could go either way. But it is up to you to go *your* way. Pick a way. Take a step. Be bold and make a decision.

Allow me to remind you of two things:

1. Ask yourself questions in order to get clear on what you want to do.
2. This decision is not etched in stone.

You may do it for a year and decide you don't love it, and you know what? That is a-okay.

The sun will still rise each morning. Just get back to work and start self-reflecting to formulate a plan as to what is next. Nursing has your back with all the options my friend, don't you worry.

Now, one point I want to make is that I don't want to make all of this seem like it's no big deal. I know it is. Trust me, I have been in this spot enough times to appreciate that, yes, in your rear view it was all a great learning experience and everything turned out fine, but, when you were in this tumultuous time, it was very stressful and overwhelming and you'd prefer not to go back to that place.

Stay calm and be patient. Get your mindset right. This is when you go back to all the tools and steps that we discussed throughout this book. Check in with your people or seek out a mentor.

For some reason, this word seems to freak people out. A mentor is simply an experienced and trusted advisor. Many times, this partnership may happen naturally, like having a great boss who mentors you while you are their employee for example. But what if you are not fortunate enough to have that? Connection is extremely personable. Sometimes two people just don't click on that level for one reason or another, and you can't just pick anyone.

Think about people you know who inspire you in your life—people you know personally or by one degree of separation (you know someone who knows them personally). That is the easiest place to start. They do not even have to be in the same field as you! If they are, of course, they would be able to understand your situation with much more context, but even if they are not, they can view things as an outsider with fresh eyes. Guidance for personal growth and motivation on some levels is pretty universal and translates across all types of jobs.

Perhaps you feel you are not ready for that or you feel like you have a decent handle on what you want to do next, but you just need to get started. You know your goal. You simply need to work backward. Let me give you a few examples.

Example – Cosmetic Nurse Practitioner: For you, your goal could be to work as an NP in a cosmetic office. If that is your final destination and right now you are a bedside nurse, you can see that we have many steps or goals ahead. This is the *most* exciting part. Because you have planned and set this goal, you can be *very* intentional on your way there. Because you know where you are headed, you can be open to recognizing opportunities, maybe even *creating* opportunities for yourself along the way.

For starters, have you ever stepped foot into one of these clinics? If not, I would say that is step one. Maybe you go to one and have a service done and chat up the nurses while you are there about the job and what it is like to work there. You might be surprised. Ask around where you work to see who knows somebody in the industry and perhaps, they can introduce you to someone willing to sit and chat with you. This can answer so many questions and be very insightful.

When I worked at the medical school, I saw several students who were 100% positive they were going to be orthopedic surgeons. They had been working their little butts off to get to the point. Their first day in the OR? Hated it.

Bummer. While I felt bad for them, I was also so happy they had that experience. Can you imagine if somehow, they were even further in their education or career and *then* decided they hated it?

Even if you feel like you know what you would want to go back to school for, if you have never been exposed to it, I urge you to take some steps *before* signing up and starting school. I have known several people that have gone back to school and graduated and ended up not wanting to pursue a job in what their degree was for.

Does this mean that school was a waste of time? Not in my opinion, as you can likely pivot and use that degree differently. But not all degrees are created equal, and I think it is fairly safe to say that few, if any, go back to school with the intent to never use their degree in some way.

On the flip side, let's say that you *know* this is the area you want to get into. You have friends that do it, you have been there, it feels like a good fit for all the right reasons – including your 'why' we discussed in the self-reflection section.

You sign up for an advanced degree program that makes the most sense for you (*so* many options these days) and off you go. So, now what do you do for the next two years while you are in school? That very much depends on you and your channel capacity. Some people may intern at a place or do some sort of side hustle in the industry while they are in school if their life allows for it.

PSA: Don't overdo it here. You need to ensure that the basics are being covered while you do this—sleeping, eating well, mentally in a good place, etc. If all that is going well, and you feel like you can take something else on, fantastic.

CHAPTER 7

Example – Non-Nursing Side Passion: Jenny loved being an ER nurse, but she also loved interior design. She worked her three twelves and went to school part-time. Breaking into the industry was tough, but eventually, she was able to work a few hours a week with a designer. When that started going well, she asked if she could go part-time at her nursing job to allow her to put more time into her design life. Her manager said yes.

Now, I know that not all managers would agree with me here, but I would rather have staff who are at work and want to be there versus the alternative. If I had told Jenny that she could not go part-time, she would likely have eventually left as she was not able to fit both loves into her life. She also would have felt unsupported by her manager. Is it a nurse manager's job to support non-nursing passions? It sure isn't. Our job is to ensure we have a unit fully staffed with competent nurses, to ensure our patients receive safe and excellent care. But in reality, we should also know that your time on the unit does not make up your entire life. As someone who has a passion for life and careers, I was always happy to help make that a reality for someone chasing a goal.

I worked through this often with my employees when I worked as a manager in the ER. I would like to think that this is where my career coaching officially started. I would meet with my staff twice a year, and although I was supposed to talk with them about modules they had yet to complete and a list of other department issues, like whether or not they were wearing their uniforms instead of Chicago Fire Department T-shirts (shout out CFD!), I spent most of the time talking to them about career plans. I knew that most of them would move on to their next challenge within a few years. This may seem counterintuitive, like I was encouraging them to leave. On the contrary, I was trying to figure out how best to support them, hoping to encourage them to stay longer.

How, you may ask? Well, as a manager, when I know what someone's interests and goals are, I'm then better able to match up opportunities with the right people. For example, if someone told me they liked informatics and helping people with our electronic health record, they may be the ones that come to mind when we have a giant project, such as moving our entire system from Cerner to Epic. Or perhaps they tell me they love teaching and are thinking about going for the educator role someday. Well, we always need preceptors; let's get you geared up and ready to take that on!

Imagine small steps that feed their creative soul while increasing staff satisfaction and benefiting the department overall. That sounds like music to a manager's ears. But here's the tricky part. Depending on the size of the staff and the department in general, this may be very hard for managers to do. If you have never been a leader/manager, let me show you what your week looks like every day:

CHAPTER 7

	Tuesday 7
6 AM	Commute to work
7 AM	
	Morning Huddle
8 AM	Check in with charge nurse about bed/plan for the day
	Meeting with your director
9 AM	
	Operations meeting
10 AM	
	Patient follow-up phone calls/emails
11 AM	
	Run to the bathroom and grab food while walking to your next meeting
12 PM	Some DMAIC project that you need to make sure everyone is doing by the end of the month
1 PM	New staff interviews because everyone keeps leaving
2 PM	Put out some fires, talk to people that come by - realize you have not drank any water
	Try to answer at least 15 of the 200 emails you have gotten today
3 PM	Go back out and check on how everyone is doing
	Security meetings about violent trauma and crowd control
4 PM	
	Service recovery for throughput issues
5 PM	Round on patients so you can brag on your staff
	Make sure nobody needs anything before you head out (they always do)
6 PM	Commute home
7 PM	
8 PM	

Essentially, you go to back-to-back meetings all day trying to find ways to eat and pee somewhere in between, come back to your desk for small amounts of time where you put out lots of unit fires, answer about fifty million emails and come to find out there is no time to actually do any of the project work that you just met about. Then, you try to get home at a decent hour to see your own family and/or have some sort of life before you do it again the next day and the next day. Oh, and you are likely on call as well. Try to get some sleep before you get paged at two in the morning.

That said, don't wait for your manager to come to you with opportunities. I wish I could tell my younger self this. "Why don't I get picked for things? Does this mean they don't think I'm good enough?" Ugh, rubbish —don't even get me started on the lecture I would give my younger self.

What your manager/boss sees is a tiny fraction of what you do every day. Why is this? Look at the calendar – they are *not there*. That said, you need to be proactive and fill in the blanks *for* them. Recognize a need for the department you are interested in and offer a solution along with yourself as someone to head it, run it, do it, whatever. This may vary depending on the size of the problem and solution, but I will give you a few real-life examples.

Example 1: Barb hated the time it took to transfer patients who were on telemetry to the multiple places they needed to go. CT, x-ray, their room, wherever. It took forever and was very disruptive to the entire unit as someone else had to watch her patients while she was gone, not to mention she would often get sick patients into her rooms when she was off the unit transporting very stable patients. This made no sense and was a huge patient safety issue. Not to mention, this was not a problem unique to Barb. This happened to all the ER nurses. She said it was like

CHAPTER 7

having pebbles in her shoe—so annoying. She wanted to fix it.

She got to work and did a literature search to better understand the risks of using central telemetry to monitor patients with the transporter in place of a nurse. She found little to no risk for adverse events in the literature. The next step was gathering data. She put binders on all of the care teams and had the primary nurses document how long they were off the unit transporting patients.

Armed with her lit search and data, she then presented her findings to various committees across the hospital including Patient Safety, Cardiology, and Quality, sharing her findings and advocating for the use of central tele for ED to inpatient transfers.

Of course, there was pushback, so she recruited a fellow ER physician (Thanks Dr. Khare!) to help advocate for her and her project. They received permission to pilot her idea and after a few weeks without any events, her dream became a reality! The pilot became the new process.

So, what was the secret sauce? She pursued something that interested her in an area she knew well that would serve her fellow nurses and the organization as a whole. That pilot pushed her to advance her education and she went on to get her Master's of Science in Healthcare Quality and Patient Safety. She used that degree to join the Performance Improvement Team over 10 years ago and is currently the Director. BOOM!

What if she did it and found out she didn't like it? No worries! She did something great for the department and then came back to continue her bedside job until the next great idea came into her mind. But she *did* love it and it started a path for her to get more involved with things. Over the years she finally made the full transition and is now managing teams that are doing what she did so long ago, systemwide. That's the thing about opportunity: it doesn't have a big neon sign attached. Most times, it looks just like regular old work -usually *more* or *extra* work, but those are opportunities that may lead you to places you didn't even know you wanted to go.

Sometimes, a shoe just fits and you keep right on walking. Toes kind of pinch? Take the lap, do it well, and then take them off in search of your next pair. Either way, you have learned so many valuable lessons along the way. You may not realize them quite yet, but I promise you have.

Maybe you are thinking, "Holy cow! That sounds amazing, but I'm not ready or motivated or (insert your word here) for all that." Let's look at another example.

Example 2: Stan loved being an ER nurse, but he was getting restless. He was busy, of course, but he wasn't feeling mentally challenged like he had been in the past. He could settle his patients with ease and on the slower days, he would go around and talk to people and tinker. One of the big issues that we found ourselves with was simple, yet hard to manage. iPhone chargers. Patients asked for them all the time, and we never had them. When the ER would buy them, patients would walk off with them, and the cycle would continue. Stan had an idea to solve this issue. He worked with Biomed to build an add-on to our video language interpreter computers which were mounted to a stand on wheels. The result was a rolling phone charger that was nearly impossible to walk off with. The whole thing cost the hospital under $10 for the materials. His angle to get the green light? Patient satisfaction, baby. *Patients are always complaining about this! How can you not have phone chargers for patients?!*

CHAPTER 7

He made a few of those interpreter/charger combos and the staff loved them as they *finally* had a solution to a very frequent complaint. That was how it started for him.

Stan liked to go around and help folks with computer issues, so when the hospital announced that they would be moving the entire system from Cerner to Epic, we knew he was one of the nurses we would ask. He became a superuser for that three-month project. He loved it and to this day is on the nursing informatics team.

The most important part is that when he was working with these folks, he understood that he was on a job interview and this was his time to shine and impress. He didn't show up and go through the motions. He was interacting with his future peers, the ones the hiring managers would ask, "What do you all think about Stan? Didn't he work on the conversion group? Should we hire him?"

He used the opportunity to network with the people in the world he considered moving into – the informatics people.

What does networking mean, anyway? I remember as a kid hearing a commercial for a shipping company and asking myself what the word 'logistics' meant. It seemed so vague and grown up. When I say 'networking' to a twenty-five-year-old, I feel like I get a similar response. Networking is not something you need to be wearing a nametag while standing in a convention center to do. Networking is simply talking to people. That's it. You may do this all the time, depending on where you fall on my chart below:

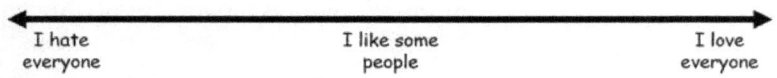

If you are on the far left there, you may struggle with this, while those on the far right are doing this all-day every day. You know the people I'm talking about. The ones that come home and say, "Honey, you are not going to believe who I ran into at the grocery store! I struck up a conversation with a lady in the bean aisle and it turns out she was married to my cousin's hairdresser's dog walker! What are the odds?!" Meanwhile, their partner is thinking, "I have never and nor will I ever speak to a stranger in the bean aisle at the grocery store."

These are the different ends of the spectrum. You likely have an idea, but if you are interested in finding where you fall, there are many types of personality-type assessments, such as the Myers-Briggs personality test (we all had to take these as hospital leaders), which may provide some insight. There are lots of free options to check out with a simple online search.

In doing these tests, I was surprised to find out that I'm social, but it takes effort. My staff and co-workers would all tell you I'm very outgoing, but this test told me that my work personality came with effort — which is true, because sometimes in my heart I feel I'm *all* the way on the left of that chart. Having this self-knowledge, I can mentally prepare for things like that conference room where I'm wearing a name badge and able to go out there and leave a great impression on those I meet. You never know what will come out of those chance encounters – and if you ask me and my rose-colored glasses, that is pretty exciting!

Life is one giant job interview of sorts...

I know what I'm about to say is going to stress half of you out and motivate the other half, but it's so true you need to hear it. People say things all the time to the effect of, "It's a small world" or "six degrees of separation," etc. This is true, and it can affect you in ways you haven't thought about. This is why it's important to keep that fact in the back of your mind and to try to be the best version of yourself when you're out there in the world doing your thing.

Think about the impression you leave on others. Of course, we do not put our 100% best self out there every moment of every day, but be mindful of the impression you tend to leave not being the one you intended to. I want us all to put our best, most genuine, and authentic foot forward every day, as much as we can.

As I've said, networking is simply talking to people. Professional networking is talking to groups of people that are in the same professional world as you. I feel like people hear this word and immediately think you are trying to sell things. A used car salesman pops into their head. Not the case.

What, or who, pops into my head is a nurse I have worked with forever. Her name is Moira, and she is a force. I love talking to her about her future life plans because she is going to do amazing things, and of this I am certain. We have some things in common, and she suggested that I talk to her mom who, go figure, is also a force.

When I was talking to her mom, she suggested that I talk to her other daughter (Moira's sister) as she is currently working in healthcare coaching. See? See how that happened? Just by sharing some ideas and thoughts, I connected with two more people who have informed and inspired me in some way. Networking doesn't have to be cheesy or self-serving. I liken it to putting out good vibes and energy into the universe and getting the same in return through like-minded people.

The takeaway here is you want to network with these forces, the Moira's in your life. People who are movers and shakers, who can inspire and encourage you. I would hope that our conversations in turn leave *her* re-energized to continue on her kick-ass journey. These things take time and many moving steps, of course.

Respect the process, but follow your gut...

I really wanted to say follow your heart instead, but sometimes your heart means well but is not the most reliable. So, we can say follow your gut first and your heart second. Not as catchy, though.

Respect the process. I'm going to be the first person to tell you that, growing up, I was super impatient, and I wanted to skip and cut corners to get things done or get to the destination faster, every time.

I'm a fast test-taker, I used to drive too fast, and I feel certain things take longer than they need to. I have read countless baby and parenting books that I felt could have been summed up in a few paragraphs, and at times I wanted to just skip the warm-up and the stretching and get right to the workout. But now that I'm in my forties, I have finally realized that many of these processes exist for a reason, and how much you should respect the process depends on a few key factors.

CHAPTER 7

- Have you done this before?
- Important follow-up question – were you successful?
- Why are you on this journey?

Marathon training is a poignant example. As discussed earlier, I had never run one before and was nowhere near running shape as a new mom. I was also not mentally in the best place, feeling very overwhelmed that life as I previously knew it was over and I was now responsible for someone else for the rest of my life.

I talked to a friend of mine who has run about fifty of them, and she suggested I follow the free training schedules offered by a famous runner and running coach, Hal Higdon [EE2] . As a bonus, the charity we were running for, Friends of Prentice, automatically enrolled us in the CARA (Chicago Area Runners Association) training program as well.

I had my plan.

As someone who has been running her entire life, the training seemed silly at first. For example, one day was run one mile, the next was walk for 40 minutes. I needed to remind myself of what I had been told over and over again in regard to training injuries.

Injuries during marathon training were incredibly common, most of them coming from overtraining or trying to do too much too soon. I followed the spring training program and patted myself on the head for the seemingly small wins of running one mile. I respected the process, but I also followed my gut.

About eighteen weeks into the program, when the miles started to get longer, I developed plantar fasciitis. For anyone who has ever had it, you know it can be miserable. Continuing to run as many miles as I was 'supposed' to be running would have only made it worse. I decided to drop one of the mid-week runs and, by making that change, was able to complete the training, and gave my angry feet a bit of a rest as well. That's the thing about the process—trusting it and respecting it does not mean follow it blindly. It is a suggestion based on what has worked in the past for many people, but not necessarily the written rule of the land.

Fast forward and those six months of training, which seemed at the time like a snail inching forward, equated to feeling **so** much better mentally and physically.

Could I have skipped all the training and crossed the finish line? With a hefty amount of walking, I feel that I could have, yes. But the sense of accomplishment in having put in months of work is what will stay with me always. Not to mention the better overall health that came along with it.

Don't be afraid to pivot...

Let's say after 18 weeks of training you decide, "You know what, this just isn't for me. I wake up every day and dread this. I get zero joy from it."

I fully support you pivoting and trying something else. You gave it a go and you learned some good lessons, all of which will likely translate into other areas. I'm not one of these people who say you have to stay on the same path until it ends – to see every single thing through. Some things, yes. Others, not so much. My career shift is a perfect example of this. If

CHAPTER 7

it's important to you and you are just being lazy, I'm going to call you on that. But you truly gave something a try and it's not a good fit? I vote for not wasting any more time. Let's find the next thing. Life is short. Options are limitless.

The answer is not always that you need a new job!

A misconception many people have is that you need a new job when you find yourself less than happy. I have thought this a time or two myself and I am pleased to report that this may not be the case!

I was working from home and picking up weekend shifts in the ER. My work-from-home job was great in that I had a great team, my kids were no longer in before-and-after care at school, I officially waved goodbye to my three-hour daily commute and my dog wasn't stuck in the house all day. Life was good. But I am an *ER nurse,* and working on a computer all day did not feed my soul like being at the hospital. I would mention this to my husband, who gets up at 4 am most days to prepare his physics lesson, and he would undoubtedly say something to the effect of, "What is wrong with you?! I would kill for a job like yours!" He was right.

There were so many things that ditching my work commute did for me and our family, but I couldn't get it out of my head. For *years*, I talked about this and kicked it around in my brain, doing all the steps I go over in this book multiple times and it finally hit me after two years or so of self-reflecting and talking to trusted friends. I *didn't* need a new job. Who said your job had to give you every single thing you need? My work-from-home job gave me a life I did not think was possible, and at the end of the day, I was not completely fried like I was when I came home from the hospital. I had the mental bandwidth to pursue a passion on the side. That passion became official in October 2022.

I named her **Straight Talk, RN LLC**[1].

I have always loved talking to nurses about their careers, so why not officially do it? This was exactly what I was looking for. It fed my soul without crushing it at the same time. It had all of the perks without any of the negatives. It was something just for me and, as previously mentioned, this book is my first official product of my company.

Thank you for being a part of this journey with me by reading! I think it is important to share true, real-life examples as so many times, trying to figure out what to do with your life seems like a faraway 'X' and no path to it.

I'm hoping that by sharing some of my stories and examples of things that have happened over the last twenty years, you will gain some valuable insight into your own journey. Over time, I have come to discover that we are never truly at our final destination. We are always moving, learning, and growing. You can do all of this, even in the same job for thirty years. Think projects, certifications, side hustles, volunteering in your community, and/or whatever gets you excited and feeds your soul.

The unknown can be a bit scary...

Until you jump in and realize that in a short time it is no longer unknown. Do not let that fear stop you. Writing this book is a great example. I am a new author. My parents are not authors. I have a cousin who is a published author [EE3] and few friends that have self-published books, but for the most part, I was fairly clueless. Where to start seemed *so* daunting.

CHAPTER 7

You go online and there is no shortage of advice, and it seems like everyone is trying to sell you something with amazing results – "Go to six figures in six days!" Um. You know what they say about when something sounds too good to be true.

Social media can be great for this kind of stuff in that you can ask for recommendations from people you know. Alternatively, you can trust your gut, pick something, and go for it. That is what I did with this book, and the fact that you are reading this right now means I have crossed the finish line. Yay!

In the end, everything in life has risk—everything. Wager what you can manage and go for it. Thinking about doing something gets you nowhere. You have to *do* it. It can be small, but the key is to keep going. Keep your eyes open to how you are feeling as this process continues. Hold yourself accountable, be patient, and win those battles with yourself.

I know everyone says this, but if I can do it, so can you. Be intentional with your time. You may just surprise yourself. And when you do? You guessed it – I want to hear all about it.

Don't let this book be yet another thought without action. Pick your one thing and get going. This life as we know it is not promised.

---

[1] Come visit me @ https://straighttalkrn.com/

[EE2]www.halhigdon.com

[EE3]https://www.amazon.com/Night-Gwen-Stacy-Died/dp/0547898169/ref=sr_1_1?crid=1VYOHYW49ZAXO&keywords=the+night+gwe

n+stacy+died&qid=1697074628&s=audible&sprefix=the+night+gwen+%2Caudible%2C116&sr=1-1

Chapter 8

Epilogue – What's next for me?

Career Coaching...

My first love. Want to chat more about your future plans?

Visit my website: www.straighttalkrn.com

Or email me hello@straighttalkRN.com with "coaching" in the subject line. I have several options depending on where you are in life. I believe sometimes all you need is a whole lot of love and a little bit of straight talk :)

Online community...

I want a spot where you can hear from nurses like you who are struggling or who have figured it out! I have plans to build a section of my website where we can post jobs, hear the truth about great and not-so great places to work and share our stories. More to come as this is a work in progress.

Does this sound like something you would be interested in? Drop me a line with "online community" in the subject line and we can talk more about what you think should be included in this space!

Future podcast...

I would love to host a podcast! I would love for real nurses to call in so we can chat live about careers, struggles, ruts, trenches, wins, you name it! I have a lot to learn about how to do this before I am able to get started, but if you are interested in being a guest let me know!

Drop me a line with the word "Podcast" in the subject line and I will add you to the list!

About the Author

Liz Even has held multiple roles in the ER for close to 20 years at Northwestern Memorial Hospital in Chicago, Illinois. She cannot remember the last time she only had one job and some favorites included working at the Feinberg School of Medicine as well as her beloved Wrigley Field with the Chicago Cubs. Her favorite job advice is to always answer with "Tell me more!" when it comes to any potential opportunity. Talking to nurses about their careers has been a passion of hers forever and she believes sometimes all you need is a whole lot of love and a little straight talk. ❤

You can connect with me on:
- https://straighttalkrn.com
- https://www.facebook.com/profile.php?id=100086591202140
- https://www.instagram.com/Straighttalk_RN

Subscribe to my newsletter:
- https://straighttalkrn.substack.com

www.ingramcontent.com/pod-product-compliance
Lightning Source LLC
Chambersburg PA
CBHW060338050426
42449CB00011B/2789